CALLED TO SERVE

Celebrating Missionary Work around the World

MIKE WINDER

This book is dedicated to my outstanding mission president and his wife, Richard B. and Marsha Stamps, and to my great companions, who all put up with me and taught me so much while I was in the Taiwan Taipei Mission (February 1995–February 1997):

Brandon Fry (MTC)

S. Hugh Palmer (Bade)

Lin Wen-Chang (Bade)

Andrew M. Hill (Bade)

Jeffrey Ward (Tuchung)

Ruan Hong-Wei (Sungshan)

Aaron C. Wixom (Sungshan)

Trent Jones (Sanchung)

Matthew Monroe (Sanchung)

Jared Schaalje (Ilan)

Jonathan Aki (Ilan)

Cover design copyright © 2014 by Covenant Communications, Inc.
Published by Covenant Communications, Inc.
American Fork, Utah
For cover image copyright, see same image in interior.

Printed in China
First Printing: February 2014

20 19 18 17 16 15 14   10 9 8 7 6 5 4 3 2 1

ISBN 978-1-62108-667-3

Acknowledgments

I sincerely appreciate the many missionaries and families who sent in images for this book to become possible. I apologize that every photograph sent in did not make it, but due to space constraints, deadlines, and the need for the highest digital resolution possible many did not. It is through everyone's heartfelt submissions that this book is enveloped with the wonderful spirit of missionary work.

I want to give special appreciation to Matt Smith at LDSmissions.com, Christine Rappleye and Aaron Shill at *Deseret News/Mormon Times*, Doug Wright and Lee Lonsberry at KSL-Radio, Jeffrey Meservy at the Taylorsville Institute, and the many family and friends on e-mail and social media who all helped spread the word about my need for pictures for this project. Without each of you this would not have been accomplished, and certainly not in the time it was.

The team at Covenant Communications did a phenomenal job, as they always do, in helping to bring this book to life. I especially appreciate my talented editor, Samantha Millburn, as well as Margaret Weber-Longoria and Mark Sorenson, my amazing design team. Managing editor Kathy Gordon and marketing and rhyming guru Ron Brough were also instrumental in encouraging this book into reality. They truly are the best in the business!

I am especially grateful to my wife Karyn and my children, Jessica, Michael, John, and Grace, for all being so supportive and patient with me while I have worked on this labor of love. Karyn was especially helpful to provide her opinion on photos, organization, and captions.

I appreciate the prophetic voice of President Thomas S. Monson, who is in tune enough with the Lord's desires that he understands that now is the great time to push forward with missionary work in a way like never before. His bold announcement changing the age requirements on when missionaries can serve electrified the Church in October 2012, and was the catalyst for me to do this book and do it right away.

I could not have done this book without the sustaining power of our Father in Heaven. He lives and wants us to seek out and help our brothers and sisters return to Him. But despite His help and that of the many others listed here, I alone am responsible for any mistakes or errors in this compilation.

Mike Winder
West Valley City, Utah

Table of Contents

Frank and Randi Park send off Elder Devin Park to the Philippines Angeles Mission

Opposite: Nicaragua Managua North Mission, Courtesy Michelle Crosland Hutchings

Dedicated missionaries go wherever they are called; always finding out that their corner of the vineyard is filled with surprises and new wonders.

I'LL GO WHERE YOU WANT ME TO GO

Will you be called to bike through paths of crowds and faces,

Or ride down long roads in wide open spaces?

Longyearbyen on the islands of Svalbard is 800 miles north of the Arctic Circle and only 600 miles below the North Pole. The Gerez family members are the only Latter-day Saints there, and they worship via Internet with the Tromsø Branch in Norway.

1. Elder and Sister Garth Heer, Norway Oslo Mission, with Carlos and Emilia Gerez in Longyearbyen, Svalbard, Norway—the northernmost missionaries ever; courtesy Carlos Gerez

2. Northernmost and southernmost points for missionary work

3. Cameron Beatty and Andrew Ludwig in Ushuaia, Tierra del Fuego, Argentina— the southernmost city in the world; courtesy Laurie Ludwig

Opposite: Twenty miles a day on a bike, often over 100 degrees, Joshua Henry Nix, Arizona Tempe Mission

Oppsosite Inset: Stephanie Morris Bassett, Taiwan Taipei Mission

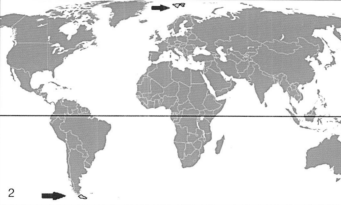

BUEN VIAJE

HASTA PRONTO

HAVE A NICE TRIP

SEE YOU SOON

Are you ready
to go to lands
wet and rainy,

And trudge
cheerfully
through floods
so insanely?

Top: Lindsey Walker, Chile Viña del Mar Mission

Bottom: Courtesy Scott Williams, Philippines Baguio Mission

Opposite: Courtesy Daniel Nifae Ah Wong, Philippines San Pablo Mission

"Whom the Lord calls,
the Lord qualifies."
—Thomas S. Monson, Apr. 1988
General Conference

5

The Russia Vladivostok Mission includes much of Siberia and some of the harshest weather on the planet, including Yakutsk, the coldest city on earth. Their average daily temperature in the winter months is -37 F (-38 C).

Are you willing to serve where for you is chosen,

Where many are cold, but few are frozen?

1. Elder Zolbayar and Elder Gary and Sister Martha Hunt at -47 F, Mongolia Ulaanbaatar Mission

2. Jordan Smith, Ukraine Donetsk Mission

3. Andrew Pettit, Russia Novosibirsk Mission

Opposite: Adam Gardner, Russia Vladivostok Mission

A frontier of
the Church,
adventure for all,

Would you go to
Africa, if that's
where you're
called?

Top: Joshua Cann, Kenya Nairobi Mission

Bottom: Tyler Albertson, South Africa Johannesburg Mission

Opposite: Grant Keaton, Mozambique Maputo Mission

8

"The truth of God will go forth boldly, nobly, and independent, 'till it has penetrated every continent, visited ever clime, swept every country, and sounded in every ear."

—Joseph Smith,
History of the Church 4:540

1. Matt Neuffer, Alpine German Speaking Mission

2. Geoffrey Tribe, Germany Munich/Austria Mission

3. Courtesy Stacey Owen, Belgium/Netherlands Mission

Opposite: At St. Basil's Cathedral in Red Square; courtesy Tyler Cecil, Russia Moscow South Mission

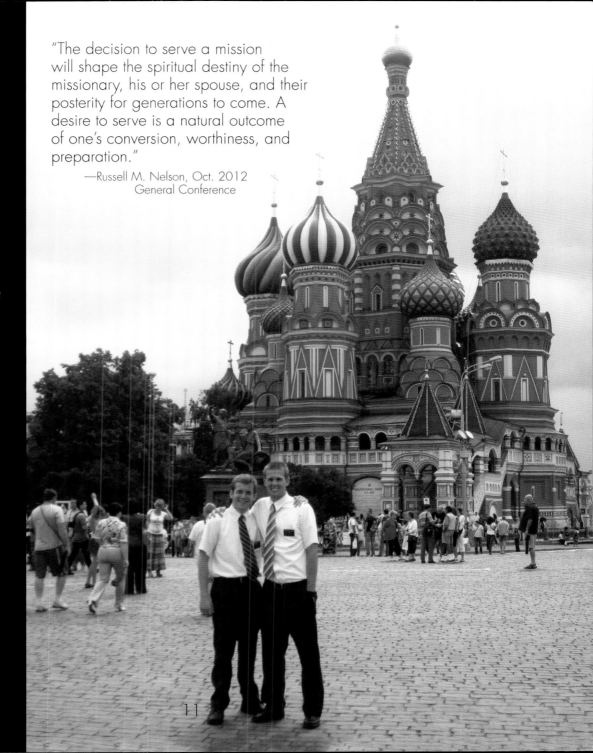

Would you serve in Europe if this is where you're called,

Where towers and traditions stand proud and tall?

"The decision to serve a mission will shape the spiritual destiny of the missionary, his or her spouse, and their posterity for generations to come. A desire to serve is a natural outcome of one's conversion, worthiness, and preparation."
—Russell M. Nelson, Oct. 2012 General Conference

11

"God is hastening His work, and He needs more and more willing and worthy missionaries to spread the light and the truth and the hope and the salvation of the gospel of Jesus Christ to an often dark and fearful world."

—Jeffrey R. Holland, *Ensign*, Nov. 2012

There are good souls to be found, regardless of which mission you're in,

Will you find them in Barcelona, Budapest, Brussels or Berlin?

1. Brett Mecham, England Leeds Mission

2. Stephen Jensen at the House of the Blackheads, Riga, Latvia, Baltic Mission

3. Courtesy Nathan Oaks, France Paris Mission

4. Courtesy Nathan Oaks, France Paris Mission

5. Victor Zanni Ruiz in Venice, Italy Milan Mission

Opposite: Leaning Tower of Pisa; courtesy Victor Zanni Ruiz, Italy Milan Mission

Will you be
called to
Asia and
serve in
that land,

Ancient,
mysterious,
crowded
and grand?

1. Matthew Monroe at the Taipei Opera House, Taiwan Taipei Mission

2. Gyeongbokgung Palace in Seoul; courtesy Anna Speegle, Korea Daejeon Mission

3. Elder Joshua Matson and Elder Dunn, Japan Nagoya Mission

4. Jared Schaalje, Taiwan Taipei Mission

"We encourage all young men who are worthy and who are physically able and mentally capable to respond to the call to serve. . . . We assure the young sisters of the Church that they make a valuable contribution as missionaries, and we welcome their service."

—Thomas S. Monson, Oct. 2012 General Conference

Russell Christensen, Japan Tokyo Mission

There were 38,321 missionaries called in the Church's first 100 years. There were more than that called in 2013 alone.

Dan McKay at the Taj Mahal, India Bangalore Mission

Or will you not be in Asia, but the Pacific you'll see,

The lands Down Under, or swaying palm tree?

1. Sister missionaries from the Australia Sydney North and Australia Sydney South Missions aboard the Manly Ferry

2. Michael Harken, South Korea Pusan Mission

3. Courtesy Andrew Jones, Australia Sydney North Mission

Will you find aloha, the warm island breeze,

Or wearing lavalava far in the South Seas?

1. Courtesy Matthew Wihongi, Tonga Nuku'alofa Mission

2. John Meyer on Yap Island, Micronesia Guam Mission

3. Elder Ioelu; Courtesy Johnny Kaio Paice, New Zealand Wellington Mission

Opposite: Warner Nielsen, Hawaii Honolulu Mission

"But great are the promises of the Lord unto them who are upon the isles of the sea."

—2 Nephi 10:21

Latin America is growing,
the Church there
is booming,

Is a future of learning
Spanish or Portuguese
looming?

Left: Sister Vargas; courtesy Aubrey Kirkham Bjork, Uruguay
Montevideo Mission

Right: Kevin Bell, Chile Santiago North Mission

Opposite: Kaitlin Blocker, Ecuador Guayaquil South Mission

The highest branch in the Church is high up in the Andes Mountains in Potosi, Bolivia (13,420 feet, or 4,090 meters above sea level).

Tijuana, Tobago, Buenos Aires or Belize,

So many places with missionary needs!

Top: Samuel Thomsen Clark, Brazil Recife Mission

Bottom: Courtesy Wyatt Ercanbrack, Guatemala Guatemala City Center Mission

Opposite: Spencer Smith, Mexico Mexico City West Mission

Over half of all missionaries are called to serve in six countries: the United States, Brazil, Mexico, Philippines, Argentina, and Peru.

Is North America
the place you
ought to be,

The home of the
brave, the land
of the free?

The first missionaries sent outside the United States were elders sent to Canada in 1833. Future Church President John Taylor was part of the large group that joined the Church as a result.

1. Sisters Jackson, Rogers, and Garcia, U.S. Capitol, Washington D.C. North Mission; courtesy Jennifer Jackson Parker

2. Logan Sisam in front of Château Frontenac in Quebec City, Canada Montreal Mission

3. Courtesy Renee Senger Layton, Kentucky Louisville Mission

4. Joseph Smith Birthplace Memorial, Sharon, Vermont; courtesy Corey Rushton New Hampshire Manchester Mission

Opposite: Sisters Call and Jensen, Florida Jacksonville Mission; courtesy Kember Call

"If ye have desires to serve God ye are called to the work; for behold the field is white already to harvest."

—Doctrine & Covenants 4:3–4

26

Modesto, Miami, Milwaukee, or Maine,

Will you serve in the Rockies or on the Great Plains?

1. Jordan Dale White, Missouri St. Louis Mission

2. Michael Garlick, Texas Dallas Mission

3. Sam Fisher in Star Valley, Wyoming, Utah Ogden Mission

4. Trenton Marck Gates, Florida Tampa Mission

Opposite: Courtesy Kaitlin Gray, New York New York South Mission

Will you go
where He wants
you to go,

Whether
mountain or
plain or sea?

Joshua Henry Nix, Arizona Tempe
Mission

Opposite: Courtesy John Pipes, Mexico
Torreón Mission

The Lord has always sent his servants out two by two, and an important part of mission life is living with a companion 24 hours a day. Together you will help each other, protect each other, and sometimes even bother each other! You will pray together, eat together, travel together, teach together, and laugh together.

TWO BY TWO

"In the mouth of two
or three witnesses
shall every word be
established."
—2 Corinthians 13:1

1. Courtesy Casey Hoyt,
Argentina Salta Mission

2. Elders Thompson and
Jensen in Latvia; courtesy
Stephen Jensen, Baltic
Mission

3. Courtesy Kelly Owen,
Romania/Moldova Mission

4. Courtesy Eugene Johnston
Awiagah, Nigeria Port
Harcourt Mission

5. Elders Furtado and
Thurgood; courtesy Daniel
Thurgood, Cape Verde Praia
Mission

6. Courtesy Hattie Cheng,
Canada Toronto West
Mission

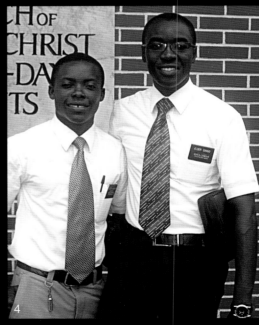

Can you
get along
with others,
companions,
districts,
zone?

They become
your family,
a home away
from home.

Are you ready to live with someone 24/7,

United in bringing souls back to heaven?

"Clean, clear, bright-eyed missionaries, laboring two-by-two, have become a living symbol of this Church everywhere. They themselves are the first gospel message their investigators encounter—and what a message that is."

—Jeffrey R. Holland, Apr. 2004 General Conference

1. Courtesy Adjo Elisabeth Aka, Louisiana Baton Rouge Mission

2. Courtesy Mika Fonoimoana, Bolivia Santa Cruz Mission

3. Sisters Klemm and Jackson prepare to teach about apostasy and restoration; courtesy Jennifer Jackson Parker, Texas McAllen Mission

4. Elly Bandeira and Karyn Hermansen Winder, Brazil São Paulo Interlagos Mission

5. Mike Winder and Ruan Hong Wei, Taiwan Taipei Mission

6. Elders Bassett and Curtis; courtesy Max Bassett, Spain Barcelona Mission

Opposite: Courtesy Junior Au, Papua New Guinea Port Moresby Mission

"Ever since the Lord sent out His disciples two by two, companionships have advanced the work of the Kingdom."

—Joseph B. Wirthlin, Oct. 1997 General Conference

34

Are you ready to ride, cruising two by two,

Helping each other in all that you do?

1. Courtesy Michelle Crosland Hutchings, Nicaragua Managua North Mission

2. Courtesy Lindsey Palmer, Bolivia Cochabamba Mission

3. Elders Lomibao and North; courtesy Carl North, California Arcadia Mission

Opposite: Joshua Anderson and Luis Goncalves, Brazil Belem Mission

And after your days together in the mission field end,

Will you discover you have made a lifelong friend?

"And ye shall go forth in the power of my Spirit, preaching my gospel, two by two, in my name, lifting up your voices as with the sound of a trump, declaring my word like unto angels of God."

—Doctrine and Covenants 42:6

Courtesy Carolyn Everton, Belgium/Netherlands Mission

Opposite: Missionaries clean up after Hurricane Sandy; courtesy Kelly Rogers, New York New York North Mission

In addition to proselyting, full-time missionaries spend hours each week providing selfless Christian service to those in need. The activities vary from volunteering at a senior center to helping after a natural disaster. For those who are called to serve, true service becomes an important part of their mission.

WHEN YE ARE IN THE SERVICE

"Our great need, our great calling, is to bring to the people of this world the candle of understanding to light their way out of obscurity and darkness and into the joy, peace, and truths of the gospel."
—Spencer W. Kimball, *Ensign* Feb. 1983

Whether helping
outdoors or fixing a tire,

Will you learn that
service's joys never
expire?

1. Sisters Reed and Larson preparing a chicken coop;
courtesy Clare Reed, Montana Billings Mission

2. Courtesy Austin Morris, Massachusetts Boston Mission

3. Courtesy Evan Parker, Texas Houston Mission

4. Helping a family cleanup after a house fire; courtesy
Jantzen Hunsaker, Florida Tallahassee Mission

Opposite: Courtesy Britton Birtcher, Russia Novosibirsk
Mission

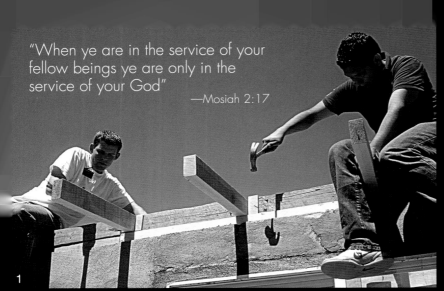

"When ye are in the service of your fellow beings ye are only in the service of your God"

—Mosiah 2:17

1. Courtesy Pablo Ramirez, Mexico Hermosillo Mission

2. Elders James and North lending helping hands; courtesy Carl North, California Arcadia Mission

3. Elders Peet and Harward help villages flooded by the Danube

4. Beth Cook, Guatemala Guatemala City Central Mission

Opposite: Courtesy Logan Sherman, Paraguay Asunción North Mission

Are you willing
to paint for
those in need,

And see how
colorful service
can be?

When working for others you just can't help but smile,

Because those good feelings will last for a while!

Eva Neves and Marlee Redford on Reunion Island, Madagascar Antananarivo Mission

Opposite: Courtesy Anna Joy Roueche, Korea Daejeon Mission

Missionaries are not just armed with the Bible but also with the Book of Mormon: Another Testament of Jesus Christ. This book has the power to bring people unto Christ, build testimonies of the restored gospel, and to change lives. Wise missionaries learn the conversion power of the spirit of this sacred record.

FLOOD THE EARTH WITH THE BOOK OF MORMON

"Please do not take the Book of Mormon for granted. Pray for a vision of how the Book of Mormon can be used more effectively in your mission."

—Joseph B. Wirthlin, Seminar for New Mission Presidents, 23 June 1999

1. Courtesy Lindsey Palmer, Bolivia Cochabamba Mission

2. A giant book used in a play put on by missionaries; courtesy Dallas Aguilar, Mexico Guadalajara Mission

3. Kelly Owen, Romania/Moldova Mission

4. Courtesy Robbie Maughn, Georgia Atlanta Mission

In Spanish,
Romanian,
French, or
Chinese,

Can you share
this good book
with a world in
need?

Top: Courtesy Elizabeth Mondragón Talavera, Mexico Mexico City West Mission
Bottom: Cameron Tribe, Ghana Accra Mission

The entire Book of Mormon has been translated in over 88 languages, including most recently in Guarani (an indigenous language of Paraguay), Sinhali (spoken in Sri Lanka), and Yaruba (spoken in West Africa).

The Church is true,
the book is blue,

Will these sacred
verses change lives,
thanks to you?

1. Elders Monson and Rogers, California Anaheim Mission; courtesy Bobi Rush

2. Josh Wihongi, Mexico Torreón Mission

3. Courtesy Jeremy Phillip Unitt, Honduras Tegucigalpa Mission

4. Madeline Jeanfreau, New York Rochester Mission

Oppostie: Dallan Carter, Mexico Torreón Mission

With missionaries on six continents, it is inevitable that they often come across not just fellow children of God but also many of our Heavenly Father's magnificent creations in the animal kingdom. The critters throughout the globe add variety and character to any mission!

UNTO EVERY CREATURE

"He who notes the sparrow's fall will, in His own way, acknowledge us."

—Thomas S. Monson, Oct. 2008 General Conference

Will you teach everyone, whether shaggy or not,

and tell them the joy that the gospel has wrought?

Top: Tyler Albertson, South Africa Johannesburg Mission

Bottom: Wade Lindley, Australia Sydney Mission

Oppostie: Steven Delgado, Mongolia Ulaanbaatar Mission

Can you navigate lizards, critters and birds,

As you go about to share the Lord's words?

1. Kevin Bell, Chile Santiago North Mission
2. Daniel Nifae Ah Wong, Philippines San Pablo Mission
3. Michael Shearer, Colombia Bogotá Mission
4. Aaron Rieske, Paraguay Asunción North Mission
5. Courtesy Nathan Kunzler, Honduras San Pedro Sula Mission
Opposite: Kaitlin Blocker, Ecuador Guayaquil South Mission

"O that I were an angel, and could have the wish of mine heart, that I might go forth and speak with the trump of God, with a voice to shake the earth, and cry repentance unto every people!"

—Alma 29:1

51

From llamas in the Andes to ducks on a farm,

Will you find joy in the journey, your smile always warm?

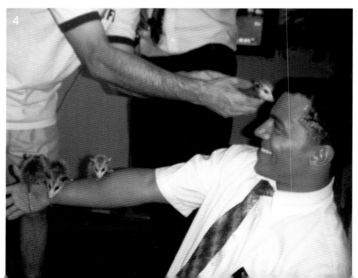

1. Preston Stocks, California Arcadia Mission
2. Kyle Riches, Chile Santiago Mission
3. Courtesy Juliette Wardle, Peru Lima Central Mission
4. Brett Hardman, Alabama Birmingham Mission

"The missionary work of the Latter-day Saints is the greatest of all the great works in all the world."

—Heber J. Grant, Oct. 1921 General Conference

Top: Courtesy Mark Carter, Uganda Kampala Mission

Bottom: Emily Sorensen Beck, Texas Houston South Mission

Can you roar like a lion in preaching out there,

Work swift as a cheetah, show courage of a bear?

1. Joshua Gourley, Brazil Curitiba Mission

2. Travis Hathcock, Oregon Eugene Mission

3. Taylor Cooper, Nicaragua Managua Mission

4. Chad Baxter, North Carolina Charlotte Mission

Opposite: Courtesy Eric Collyer, Kenya Nairobi Mission

"We accept the responsibility to preach the gospel to every person on earth. And if the question is asked, 'You mean you are out to convert the entire world?' the answer is, 'Yes. We will try to reach every living soul.'"

—Boyd K. Packer, Oct. 1975 General Conference

Don't worry
about missing
your dog or
your cat,

Animals will
abound in
the mission
you're at!

Sisters Maren Wilson and Kelsey
Edwards, Alabama Birmingham Mission

Opposite: Jacob Haltom, Zimbabwe
Harare Mission

Missionaries love when people are humble, teachable, and childlike. Perhaps this is why children in the mission field easily capture the hearts of missionaries—many of whom miss siblings of their own back home. These little friends have a way of brightening a day and often provide the encouragement to their parents to embrace the Church.

SUFFER THE LITTLE CHILDREN

"There is a way to reach every human heart, and it is your business to find the way to the hearts of those to whom you are called on your mission."
—Lorenzo Snow, *Improvement Era* Dec. 1899

1. Courtesy Matthew Wihongi, Tonga Nuku'alofa Mission

2. Steve Densley, California Sacramento Mission, Hmong Speaking

3. Courtesy of Ev Cann, Kenya Nairobi Mission

4. Brad Royal, Philippines Angeles Mission

Are you willing to be looked up to by the tiny,

Ensuring that your example is always shiny?

Top: Pierce Kenworthy, Argentina Rosario Mission

Bottom: Sisters Wendoline Vang and Sharon Torres, Utah Salt Lake City West Mission

The first single, proselyting sister missionaries were Inez Knight and Lucy Jane (Jennie) Brimhall, assigned to serve in Great Britain in 1898.

Will you show the children how to pray,

Prepare them to be missionaries themselves someday?

1. Courtesy Grant Keaton, Mozambique Maputo Mission
2. Courtesy Aaron Perrell, Brazil São Paulo South Mission
3. Michael Christensen, Honduras San Pedro Sula Mission

Opposite: Sisters Reed and Aiken teach prayer with "prayer rocks"; courtesy Clare Reed, Montana Billings Mission

It would be a mistake to think that the highly structured environment of a mission stifles any sense of humor. Quite the opposite! Missionaries enjoy a good laugh, a fun pose for the camera, and the lighter moments that keep life enjoyable. Missions are filled with good times!

HE DID SMILE UPON THEM

May the force be with you, and you'll go far.

Be that superhero your mom thinks you are!

1. Sisters Walker and Shumway; Courtesy Lindsey Walker, Chile Viña del Mar Mission

2. Michael Young, Germany Frankfurt Mission

3. Eugene Johnston Awiagah, Nigeria Port Harcourt Mission

Opposite: Daniel Macias, England London Mission

"The spirit of the gospel will shine forth from their souls and others will partake of their light and rejoice therein."

—Joseph F. Smith, Apr. 1899
General Conference

Top: Courtesy James Dee Boatman, Canada Edmonton Mission

Bottom: Katie Edwards Robison, Dominican Republic Santo Domingo West Mission

The elders are sometimes goofy, the sisters stop for fun;

Are you ready to enjoy the journey until your work is done?

Top: Courtesy Jack Kohler, Arkansas Little Rock Mission

Bottom: Steven Hermansen, Texas Dallas Mission

"There is a way for everyone—even the hesitant missionary—to participate in this great work. We can each find a way to use our own particular talents and interests in support of the great work of filling the world with light and truth."

—Dieter F. Uchtdorf, *Ensign*, Feb. 2013

Will you jump for joy with the good news,

That right will triumph, and wicked will lose?

Daniel Jenson, France Paris Mission

1. Joshua Anderson popping a backflip right on the equator, Brazil Belem Mission

2. Courtesy Russell Christensen, Japan Tokyo Mission

3. Courtesy Joshua Henry Nix, Arizona Tempe Mission

4. Courtesy Hattie Cheng, Canada Toronto West Mission

Can you find the right balance between hard work and play,

Allowing the sunshine to brighten your day?

1. Can't quite reach the doorbell! Courtesy Dallan Carter, Mexico Torreón Mission

2. Travis Hathcock, Oregon Eugene Mission

3. Courtesy Jordan Smith, Ukraine Donetsk Mission

4. Madison VanDenBerghe, New York Rochester Mission

Opposite: Courtesy Philip Barr, Texas San Antonio Mission, Spanish Speaking

THE CHURCHES OF CLIFTON SPRINGS WELCOME YOU

First Baptist Church

Church of the Nazarene

United Methodist Church

St. Felix Catholic Church

St John's Episcopal Church

Orson Pratt, a member of the Council of the Twelve from 1835 to 1881, served more missions than anyone in Church history. His 19 full-time missions included 16 crossings of the Atlantic Ocean by ship.

"The Lord has not chosen the great and learned of the world to perform his work on the earth but humble men and women devoted to his cause."
—Lorenzo Snow, *Deseret Weekly* 57:513

Will you make events fun, look forward to mail,

Smile with the locals, and never despair?

Opposite: Courtesy Amanda Welch, Young Performing Missionary, Illinois Nauvoo Mission)

1. Courtesy Russell Christensen, Japan Tokyo Mission

2. Brady Leavitt, Thailand Bangkok Mission

3. Thrilled to get an avalanche of "Dear Elder" letters, Jordan Royal, Philippines Angeles Mission

Along your way, will you look for the good,

Find things to laugh about, grin when you should?

1. Courtesy Anna Joy Roueche, Korea Daejeon Mission

2. Thomas Larsen, Oakland Temple grounds, California Santa Rosa Mission

3. Steven Hermansen, Texas Dallas Mission

4. Courtesy Kenard Beckford, Alabama Birmingham Mission

Opposite: Courtesy Emily Beck, Utah Salt Lake City Temple Square Mission

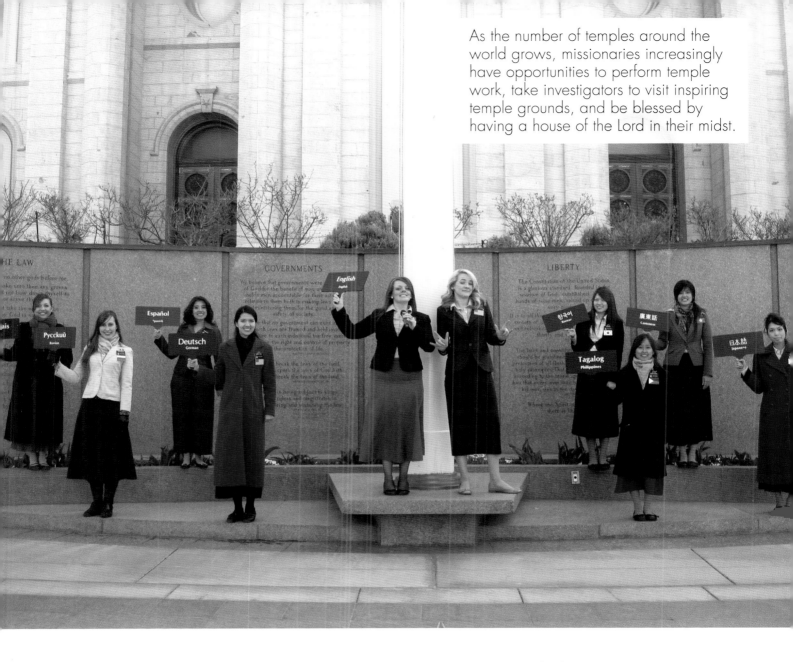

As the number of temples around the world grows, missionaries increasingly have opportunities to perform temple work, take investigators to visit inspiring temple grounds, and be blessed by having a house of the Lord in their midst.

I LOVE TO SEE THE TEMPLE

Can you share the peace the temple gives,

With those you teach, that God still lives?

The Preston England Temple was built in the area in part to commemorate the first missionaries to Great Britain that taught in the town of Preston and baptized in the nearby River Ribble. In the 1850s there were more Saints in Europe than America.

1. Seoul Korea Temple; courtesy Kenneth Bacarro, Korea Seoul Mission

2. Rome Italy Temple under construction; courtesy Brandon Lemmon, Italy Rome Mission

3. Billings Montana Temple; courtesy Lindsay Tuckett, Montana Billings Mission

4. Tonga Temple; courtesy Jacob Michael, Tonga Nuku'alofa Mission

5. Italian-bound missionaries at the Provo Utah Temple; courtesy Victor Zanni Ruiz, Italy Milan Mission

6. Elders Keaton and Payne at Curitiba Brazil Temple; courtesy Ben Keaton, Brazil Curitiba Mission

7. Los Angeles Temple; courtesy Cameron Huffaker, California San Fernando Mission

8. Manhattan New York Temple; courtesy Kaitlin Gray, New York New York South Mission

9. Mexico City Temple; courtesy Sergio Ammon Alvarez Rangel, Mexico Tuxtla Gutierrez Mission

10. Guayaquil Ecuador Temple; courtesy Kaitlin Blocker, Ecuador Guayaquil South Mission

Will you, like the angel, sound the horn,

That Christ's ancient Church has been reborn?

1. Guatemala Temple; courtesy Beth Cook, Guatemala City Central Mission

2. Tegucigalpa Honduras Temple; courtesy Jeremy Phillip Unitt, Honduras Tegucigalpa Mission

3. São Paulo Brazil Temple; courtesy Margaret Yorgason Rappleye, Brazil São Paulo Interlagos Mission

4. Toronto Ontario Temple; Courtesy Spencer Ficiur, Canada Toronto West Mission

Opposite: Montevideo Uruguay Temple, Courtesy Aubrey Kirkham Bjork, Uruguay Montevideo Mission

The farthest mission headquarters from any temple in the Church is the mission home in Bangalore, India. Its closest temple is in Hong Kong, China, 2,486 miles (4,000 kilometers) away.

Is it worth being away
from your family
for a time,

So that other families
can be with theirs
for eternity?

Right: Taipei Taiwan Temple; courtesy Nicole Dowdle Keaton,
Taiwan Taipei Mission

Left: Washington D.C. Temple; courtesy Jennifer Jackson
Parker, Washington D.C. North Mission

Opposite: Lunch in Malta; courtesy Brandon Lemmon, Italy
Rome Mission

Missionaries do feast upon the word of God, but their appetite for real food is often insatiable. Between home-cooked member meals, exotic local fare, or mystery companion cooking, the dining aspect of a mission adds a delicious dimension to any mission experience!

AND THEY DID EAT

1. Sisters Gomez and Barber; courtesy Ines Gomez, Texas Dallas Mission

2. Elders Ganley and Boatman; courtesy James Dee Boatman, Canada Edmonton Mission

3. Travis Petersen, Brazil Campinas Mission

4. Austin Ercanbrack, Brazil Belo Horizonte Mission

5. Cody Bracken, Missouri St. Louis Mission

Opposite: Anna Joy Roueche, Korea Daejeon Mission

"Blessed are they which do hunger and thirst after righteousness: for they shall be filled."
—Matthew 5:6

Are you ready for food you never knew existed,

Cooking a bit, and doing your own dishes?

81

There are over 2,200 pounds of Lucky Charms cold cereal consumed by missionaries each month at the Provo Missionary Training Center.

1. Mandarin Chinese learning missionaries practice their chopsticks in the Provo Missionary Training Center; courtesy Mike Winder

2. Courtesy Aubrey Kirkham Bjork, Uruguay Montevideo Mission

3. Jennifer Nielson Scott, China Hong Kong Mission

4. Elder Alshengti's birthday; courtesy Bobi Rush, California Anaheim Mission

Can you find
pizza in the spot
that you land,

Gelato, great
burgers, or
mystery flan?

Top: Italian gelato enjoyed by Victor
Zanni Ruiz, Italy Milan Mission

Bottom: Courtesy Kelly Rogers, New
York New York North Mission

Missionaries develop a genuine, heartfelt love for the people of their mission. As they labor to teach and serve them, they build sweet relationships and lifetime friendships. They also encounter some remarkable and interesting people along the way!

MINISTERING AMONG MY PEOPLE

Oh the people you meet in the places you'll go,

Are you ready for humanity's wonderful show?

Opposite: Joseph Bjork, Belgium/Netherlands Mission

1. Madison VanDenBerghe, New York Rochester Mission

2. Andy Nelson contacting atop Sugarloaf Mountain, Brazil Rio de Janeiro Mission

3. Sisters Mills and Yashenkova with new member; courtesy Robert Hokanson, Ukraine Kiev Mission

"If we do not do our duty in regard to missionary service, then I am convinced that God will hold us responsible for the people we might have saved had we done our duty."

—Spencer W. Kimball, *Ensign* Oct. 1977

1. Courtesy Andrew Pettit, Russia Novosibirsk Mission

2. Elders Olson and Mortinsen, Thailand Bangkok Mission

3. Courtesy Grant Keaton, Mozambique Maputo Mission

4. Courtesy Junior Au, Papua New Guinea Port Moresby Mission

Opposite: Courtesy Katie Edwards Robison, Dominican Republic Santo Domingo West Mission

The Spirit will be with you when truths you teach,

Will you love the people to whom you are sent to preach?

1. Courtesy Nkoro Essang Nkoro, Nigeria Port Harcourt Mission

2. Courtesy Nicole Dowdle Keaton, Taiwan Taipei Mission

3. Paul Kimball in St. Kitts, Puerto Rico San Juan Mission

4. Courtesy Katie Edwards Robison, Dominican Republic Santo Domingo West Mission

5. Courtesy Brandon Lemmon, Italy Rome Mission

6. Courtesy Brad Royal, Philippines Angeles Mission

Opposite: Baptism in the Indian Ocean, Grant Keaton, Mozambique Maputo Mission

Seeing children of our Heavenly Father choose to covenant with Him and come into the waters of baptism is a thrill for any missionary. Baptism must be by immersion, and from rivers to oceans, from indoor fonts to swimming pools, they are taking place all over the world every day.

HOW GREAT SHALL BE YOUR JOY

"Let them go two by two, and thus let them preach by the way in every congregation, baptizing by water, and the laying on of the hands by the water's side." —Doctrine and Covenants 52:10

1. Joshua Anderson and Luis Goncalves, Brazil Belem Mission
2. Courtesy Tyler Albertson, South Africa Johannesburg Mission
3. Courtesy John Pipes, Mexico Torreón Mission

Whether indoor
or outdoor, a pool
or the sea,

Will you help
folks obey
"Come follow me"?

1. Courtesy Jacob Haltom, Zimbabwe Harare Mission
2. Courtesy Anna Speegle, Korea Daejeon Mission
3. Courtesy Jake Mize, Mexico Tuxtla Gutierrez Mission
4. Courtesy Ines Gomez, Texas Dallas Mission

"I promise you that as you magnify your call this will be the sweetest and most glorious experience you have had."

—Ezra Taft Benson,
Teachings of Ezra Taft Benson, 205

In highlands
and lowlands,
in lochs,
streams, or
fonts,

Can you guide
souls to Jesus,
as He would
want?

1. Courtesy Jed Winder, Scotland
Edinburgh Mission

2. Courtesy Michael Shearer, Colombia
Bogotá Mission

3. All men are in kilts on Robert Burns
Day; courtesy Jed Winder, Scotland
Edinburgh Mission

Opposite: Courtesy Michelle Crosland
Hutchings, Nicaragua Managua North
Mission

Can you imagine your first baptism, people clothed in white,

When the Spirit is so palpable, countenances so bright?

Top: Courtesy Nkoro Essang Nkoro, Nigeria Port Harcourt Mission

Bottom: Baptism in the Black Sea; Courtesy Grant Harward, Romania Bucharest Mission

"Go ye into all the world, and preach the gospel to every creature. He that believeth and is baptized shall be saved."

—Mark 16:15–16

1. Kraig Dye, Puerto Rico San Juan East Mission

2. Matt Pierce, Utah Ogden Mission

3. Courtesy Renee Senger Layton, Kentucky Louisville Mission

4. Courtesy Eric Collyer, Kenya Nairobi Mission

How would
you feel on a
baptism day,

To know
you had
helped show
someone the
way?

While in Hanley,
England in 1839,
Wilford Woodruff
baptized 600 souls.
While in Wales on
two missions in the
1840s and '50s,
Dan Jones baptized
several thousand.

"And if it so be that you should labor all your days in crying repentance unto this people, and bring, save it be one soul unto me, how great shall be your joy with him in the kingdom of my Father!"

—Doctrine and Covenants 18:15

1. Courtesy Katie Edwards Robison, Dominican Republic Santo Domingo West Mission

2. Courtesy Joe Miller, Brazil Goiânia Mission

3. Elder Vargas baptizing in the Rio Grijalva, which some scholars believe to be the Book of Mormon's River Sidon, Mexico Villahermosa Mission

4.Courtesy Wyatt Ercanbrack, Guatemala Guatemala City Center Mission

"Few joys in life are sweeter and longer lasting than knowing that you have helped others take the restored gospel of Jesus Christ into their hearts."

—Henry B. Eyring,
Ensign, Feb. 2011

1. Courtesy Mark Carter, Uganda Kampala Mission

2. Courtesy Katie Edwards Robison, Dominican Republic Santo Domingo West Mission

3. Courtesy Jordan Keele, Mexico Hidalgo Mission

Will you take that dear one by the hand,

To waters leading to God's promised land?

Top: Courtesy Michelle Crosland
Hutchings, Nicaragua Managua North
Mission

Bottom: David Payne, West Indies
Mission

Missionaries work hard, and their time is rewarding and very fulfilling. They travel, train, and teach. They study, pray, and learn. And they also have to shower, do laundry, shop, and sleep.

WORK AS MISSIONARIES DO

The first deaf missionaries for the Church were two elders and four sisters set apart March 9, 1952 to labor in Ogden, Utah.

Companionship study, personal study, and language study too;

Are you ready to apply yourself, work hard in what you do?

1. Courtesy Lennart Crossley, Madagascar Antananarivo Mission

2. Courtesy Eugene Johnston Awiagah, Nigeria Port Harcourt Mission

3. Pierce Kenworthy, Argentina Rosario Mission

Opposite: Courtesy Saxon Porter, California Santa Rosa Mission

"A mission will provide a strong foundation upon which one's future life can be built. Not only will individuals be blessed as they serve missions, but the entire Church will also be strengthened."

—Thomas S. Monson,
Feb. 3, 2013 *Church News*

102

On transfer day,
will you go where the
mission president sends,

Taking buses,
trains, or planes
to reach that end?

1. Courtesy Grant Harward, Romania Bucharest Mission

2. Transfer by plane, Daniel Thurgood, Cape Verde Praia Mission

3. Transfer day, courtesy Steven Delgado, Mongolia Ulaanbaatar Mission

Opposite: Victor Zanni Ruiz, Italy Milan Mission

You may fix your bike's flat tire or adjust a loose chain,

Are you ready for laundry, showering, and life not the same?

Top: Joseph Bjork, Belgium/Netherlands Mission

Bottom: Sisters Klemm and Jackson; courtesy Jennifer Jackson Parker, Texas McAllen Mission

"There will arise from the performance of missionary duties honor, and glory and exaltation."
—Lorenzo Snow,
Deseret Weekly 50:737–738

Top: Karyn Hermansen Winder, Brazil São Paulo Interlagos Mission

Bottom: Jake Mize, Mexico Tuxtla Gutierrez Mission

Following Page: Courtesy Jack Kohler, Arkansas Little Rock Mission

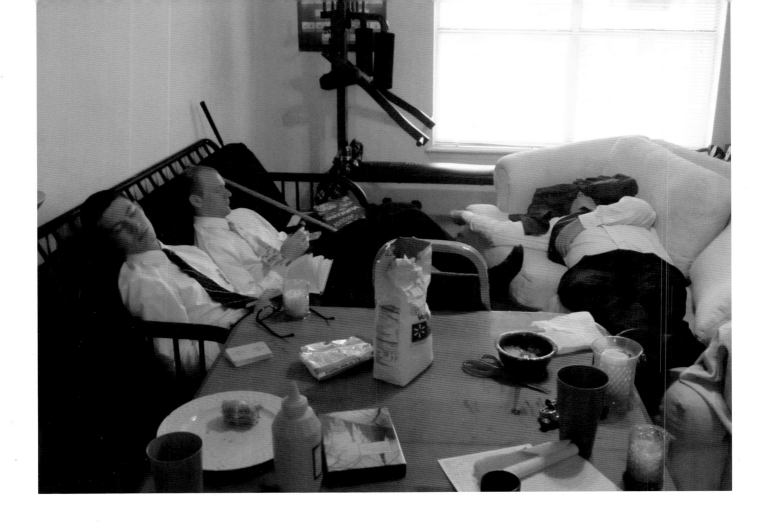

And when the day is done
and at last you find your rest,

"Well done" will say our Father,
"I'm pleased you've done your best!"